Your Free Gift

I wanted to express my appreciation that you support my work so I've put together a free gift for you

31 Healthy Smoothie recipes for month*

Just visit the link above to download it now.

I'm sure you will love this gift.

Thanks

*Link to download book
http://publish4you.wixsite.com/ebook-gift

Table of contents

Universal Body Language..5

    More Reliable than Spoken Language 8

    Notice Your Own Body Cues...9

    Notice the Effect Your Body Language Has On Others..................10

Importance of First Impression...12

    - In General 12

    - Job/Interview 13

    Date/Relationships..15

    Pickup/Negotiations...18

Personality Types and Different Behavior Patterns 21

    Extrovert vs. Introvert..21

        The difference in Personal Space: 22

        Willingness to Touch:..23

        Eye Contact:...23

        Idiosyncrasies:...24

    Liars vs. The Honest 24

        Fidgeting:..26

        Abnormal Blinking..27

        Exaggerated Gestures:...27

    The Dangerous Ones 28

        Contradictory Body Language 28

        Invasive/Forward-Learning Body Language:.................29

General Body Language Examples...30

    Feet and Legs 30

        Toes pointed away 30

Legs squeezed together 30

Crossed ankles behind them...30

Jittery Legs...31

Soles exposed...31

Chest and Shoulders..31

Crossed arms...31

Hunched shoulders 31

Puffed Chest 32

Diagonal Alignment...32

Consistent Shoulder Adjustment.....................................32

Hands and Fingers...32

White Knuckled Fist...32

Open palms 32

Wringing...33

Knuckle Cracking...33

Eye Contact...33

Consistent Downward Looks 33

Avoidance of Eye Contact - 33

Strained Eye Contact..33

Abnormal Blinking...34

Posture/Positioning..34

Curved Spine...34

Rigid Spine 34

Personal Space...34

Spreading..35

Facial Expressions 35

Eye-Involved Smiling 35

Impossible to be Disgusted with a Smile 35

True Fear 35

Gestures 36

Wild arm movement 36

Backhanded 36

Talking with Hands 36

Methods and Techniques to Analyze People............................37

Establishing the Norms Through Observation 37

Discover the Individual Body Language of Those You Know,
Associated with Situations...39

Pay Special Attention to Non-Necessary, Compulsory Body
Language e.g. fidgeting..41

Universal Body Language

One of the most important and essential languages you will ever learn is body language. It crosses many borders and can speak non-verbal volumes no matter whom you are speaking with and where on Earth you call home. Much like mathematics, body language conveys ideas and emotions in a nearly universal manner. However, that keyword - 'nearly' may just mean the difference between impressing and offending, and even life or death.

Thus, it is of great importance that we understand early on in our journey, that not all body language is universal. Some gestures that you, the reader, may intuitively associate with affirmatives may be used to convey negatives in other cultures. The importance of recognizing this is that you will, without a doubt, come across many people whose origins lie in other countries, other traditions, and other religions. In essence, your study of body language is meant to help you communicate more effectively with other people - therefore, it would be foolish for us to ignore that what works for 8/10 might backfire with the rest.

Let's detail a few of those major differences of body language between cultures:

First, probably the most surprising to beginners is that smiling is not a universal gesture of friendliness. If you are anything like most students of body language, you are quite skeptical right now, wondering how any culture could perceive the friendly smile in a negative fashion. This is because, the majority of you - those of you living in the Western parts of the world, run into people every day that wears large, bright smiles. Waitresses, cashiers, bosses and colleagues, and friendly strangers you might pass by on the street. And, you likely smile back.

In that case, it would probably surprise you to know that in Russia, for instance, smiling is seen as a very shady, questionable gesture when coming from anyone but family, friends, or love interests. Smiling in a warm, friendly way at a stranger is more likely to attract negative attention to you than the positive. Here, if we meet an unusually friendly person on the street many of us have a boost of self-esteem and happiness. In Russia, it causes skepticism and distrust.

This is because the norm in Russia is to view a smile as a show of submission. Perhaps it's the same thing here? We submit, thus using a smile to show people we mean no harm. However, in Russia, this is seen as very suspect. There is a sense that this show of benevolence is a smokescreen to hide the malice of your true intent. Maybe those of us that don't smile as much as others are of a more Russian mindset?

Other great examples are the 'thumbs up' and 'O-K' hand signals. Both are benign and even friendly gestures in the West but are more synonymous with raising the middle finger for those in the East. Best be careful of using those gestures when you are in places like Brazil, Germany, Russia, and the Middle East.

Speaking of the Middle East, we come to the last example of non-universal body language that we are going to examine. This bit of body language has been very confusing and difficult to grasp for many soldiers doing tours in Iraq, Afghanistan, and other predominantly Arabic countries.

In the West, there is a certain distance between people when speaking with one another. A good foot or two, generally. That is unless aggressions have boiled over and a fight is on the horizon - in which case, the two combative people get nearly 'nose to nose'. Getting close to someone's face is something that only happens in the West during intimacy or during a fight. This is not the case in the Middle East.

It is common for Middle Easterners to approach someone and get intimately close to them in order to speak. Not to fight, not to argue, but just to speak. They might be asking what you want to eat or how your day is going. This takes a lot of adjustment for soldiers because it is in their nature as Westerners to take an offensive stance and become defensive in response to a nose-to-nose altercation. Yet, they find that there is no altercation to be found.

Given these three examples, you may be slightly intimidated to understand body language better. After all, if innocent gestures can give off negative vibes, and seemingly dangerous posture and positioning are seen as benign, what hope do we have in understanding others better through body language?

And that is exactly why this book exists. To give you greater skill and confidence in your interactions with people from all over the world, not just your neighbors, your family, and your date. There are places on Earth where having eye contact too long can start a deadly fight, and shaking your head means 'yes'. Maybe you are thinking 'well, alright, but I don't plan to go to those places. Just tell me how to interact with people from my own culture'. The issue therein being that people are just as diverse and complicated as the different cultures around the world. Without the right tools, your body language will defy you - either telling lies or tell truths better hidden.

Our first step is to recognize the body language that is universal. You will find that, by the end of this book, not a lot is totally certain without context and analysis. But, these five particular facial cues can give away the secrets you seek no matter who you are talking to or from what culture you belong:

These cues are the ones for disgust, sadness, anger, fear, and surprise. The most reliable forms of body language are quick, subtle, and need a trained eye to notice. They are called 'micro-expressions'. How do you tell if a love interest might be into you, despite the words coming out of her mouth? How do you tell crocodile tears from genuine dismay? How can you search for anger in the face of someone trying to play it cool?

Micro-expressions, that's how. They are quick and revealing. A sobbing woman might show a micro-expression of happiness as she discovers you are buying into her fake tears, a kind-hearted person might wrinkle their nose for a split second in disgust even as she engages you in conversation and pretends not to be bothered by your advances. The key to discovering the true intentions, emotions, and thoughts of others is to learn to read the body language they are not controlling. We can all fake a convincing facial expression if we try hard enough, but a trained eye can still discover the behind-the-scenes secrets in the quick lapses in our act.

More Reliable than Spoken Language

If we were to put that in terms of spoken language, we would call micro-expressions 'Freudian slips': which is a phenomenon in which a person accidentally speaks their true, transparent thoughts before returning to the view they are trying to express. Our mind knows what the truth is, and it knows what our smokescreen version of the truth is. However, the more we are put under pressure and/or the more versions of the truth we create, we make it much more plausible to have a 'leak' in the pipes that are our neural connections. In other words, your mind and body are more honest than you are and they will betray you from time to time as you try to peddle your lies.

This is why reading body language is more reliable than wholeheartedly believing spoken word. Even the most honest person hides truths from themselves. The disconnect between the subconscious and conscious mind can be significant, even in someone not intending to deceive. For instance, a friendly person does not want to consider that they don't want to stand and talk to you all day about your cats, but you can still observe, from their body language, that they are less than intrigued with your story about Fluffy hacking up a hairball. Subconsciously, his feet may point away from you - so might his body. His head will face you, and he may be aware enough to nod his head and have strong eye contact - but, the signs are there that he'd really rather be somewhere else right now. Probably anywhere else.

Learning how to read body language isn't all about catching people in lies. Sometimes people just have to hide their preferences, emotions, and intent because it is what is best for them. How many salesmen do you think to hop up and down when they hear a significant amount of money being offered for what they are selling? If they think they can get an even better deal, then they will do their best to do so - but, they won't accomplish that if they show how happy they are with your very first offer. We will get more into why your boss has to portray particular body language in a job interview later, and we will detail why you might have a better chance with your crush than you think - despite their appearance of indifference.

Notice Your Own Body Cues

There is no better test dummy to learn how to read body language than yourself. While you don't look at yourself all day in the mirror, so will likely miss out on micro-expressions, you can still observe how your body language changes depending on the situation or the tone of conversation/interaction. Notice the times where you automatically cross your arms, and then notice when you have got your arms and legs spread out and your body language is open as can be. What's the difference? What are you feeling at those times?

A great way to get started is to talk to your reflection in the mirror - imagining it is someone else. Purposely try to ooze confidence, purposely try to look insecure. Imagine you are arguing, then argue your side - use words you think are really cutting and mean. Then try imagining that you are trying to soothe someone who is upset and reassure them. As you are doing all of these things, try to observe your body language. The gestures, facial expressions, and posture that you'll use when trying to be confident will be far removed from the body language you use to let out your vulnerability. By observing your body language in this way, you accomplish two important things. 1) You develop a basic understanding of the body language others might use in those given situations, thus you will be able to see the situations coming before they arrive - body language tends to start telling the story before any words are even spoken, and 2) You will begin to have a complete view of what body language you, yourself, use in those given situations. This is very important - as learning to understand body language is not all about being able to read and analyze others, but also learning how to use your own body language for better communication and success.

It may take several practices of this exercise before you have a purer grasp of what your body language is like. Often, when we start 'acting 'or 'trying' we overdo what we would do naturally. The more you practice, however, the more relaxed you will become and the more the illusion of speaking to someone else - rather than your own reflection - will come to life.

Notice the Effect Your Body Language Has On Others

In the next chapter, we will be discussing the effect body language has on first impressions; when you are meeting someone for the first time, when you are looking to get a job or a date. By far, the most essential thing you can take to heart from this book is that more than your words ever will, your body language can assure particular treatment from others. The only question is - will your body language assure positive treatment or negative treatment?

A good jokester can use even the meanest, insulting words and still flatter and charm others through the power of their body language. If you want to be able to influence, persuade, express, and communicate well through text and email, this book isn't going to be what you need. However, if you want to learn how to influence, persuade, express, and communicate well in the real world - face to face - where it matters, then you had best pay particular attention to every lesson listed in this text.

A master of body language need only use a few words to convey an essay worth of meaning. These are the confident men and women that walk into job interviews with the least amount of applicable experience and yet manage to leave the bosses office, not only with the job they applied for, but with the boss left impressed, charmed, and looking forward to having them in the workplace. The master of body language can walk into a room full of chattering, clever pickup artists and command all the female attention while speaking few words and being comparatively indifferent to their attraction.

To begin the journey to mastering this language, you must open your eyes wider. Observe how your body language affects people. How does a chatty person react when you suddenly cross your arms and break eye contact? Meanwhile, how does a quiet person react when you open up, look at them, and gently initiate conversation? The more you understand your own ability to manipulate situations based upon your body language, the more you will see through the body language of others and see their true feelings and intent. Be curious and you will notice what most people don't see. Use these secrets and achieve what most people cannot.

Importance of First Impression
- In General

Are first impressions impossible to overcome? No. But, it is extraordinarily difficult. This is why so many experts in body language, communication, negotiation, pickup, and dating will emphasize the importance of a good first impression. There is a lot that goes on in a first meeting. First and foremost, people begin making quick judgments about each other within the first few seconds of meeting. These judgments can often be overridden by later experiences, but an ineffectual first impression will assure only one thing: that you will be quickly forgotten.

Weird as it may seem, a good first impression does not always mean coming off as a 'good person' or expressing yourself in a fully fleshed-out way. There is a limit to what we can retain in a first meeting - partially because we don't really care all that much about the little, intimate details of a stranger. All that fun comes later. A good first impression is achieved by assuring that you leave an impression at all. Make them think of you even after you have left, and you have succeeded. Every other opinion of you can be adjusted later, you only fail if no opinion is ever formed. People have to care in order to form opinions about you. That is why, through your words - but more through your body language - you have to make an impact and make them care.

The simple truth is that the majority of strangers are immediately on the defensive when meeting someone new. Yes, even the ones that claim to love meeting new people. it is because humans are pack animals - we are able to become very fond and loving with those we know, but we are defensive and on alert when we come across someone new. People fear what they don't know. That's all true, and it describes human nature. A nature, by the way, that you can overcome through the art of body language.

In the next few examples, we will go over the dos and don'ts of first impression body language and how to increase your chances of making an impression and having success in communications and negotiations. All body language teachings need to be applied to their context. Certain gestures can be helpful in some situations and detrimental in others. Very much like the cultures of different countries can massively affect the efficacy of different forms of body language, so too can a shift in the situation.

Below, we will go over how to adjust for professional environments, how to optimize for success on dates and in relationships, and how to improve your luck in pickup situations as well as during negotiations. There is a lot of overlap in all these situations, which will hopefully help to teach you how all language - including body language - is interaction based. No words or gestures stand on their own, they must be put into context and into the proper situations in order to derive their power.

- Job/Interview

On the surface, most people would believe that a boss has more resistance to offering a job than a man or woman would have to go on a date. Especially when factoring in the fact that your work is going to be traded for money, and no boss in their right mind is going to throw money at someone that they don't think can do the job they are hiring them for. Strangely, however, it turns out to be the opposite. Some of you reading this will find this obvious, but you may not be putting the implications into good use.

When you have been brought in for a job interview, your application has already been reviewed and your chances of getting the job are significantly higher than those that applied but did not hear back. In fact, it is often the case that the job interview is more of a formality than you might imagine. What they are truly trying to accomplish is to see if the asset they predict you to be is squared up with who you truly are. In other words, the job interview isn't an opportunity to battle for the job, it is an opportunity to prove yourself to be as great as they already believe you are.

Yet, very few people approach a job interview with this mindset. They become very worrisome and insecure, worrying about if they will be able to answer the questions properly or if they won't be liked. Whereas the fact is, they contacted you because they already think you'd be a pretty good fit. No one expects you to be an expert at the job they are offering before you get the job in the first place. They expect you to show an aptitude for learning and an excitement for the job.

Your potential boss has, metaphorically, read the book blurb on your cover and is ready to read. All you have to do is expand a bit more on what they already know. You don't have to prove yourself at this point. Often, those that enter a job interview with insecurity and low self-esteem will actually portray a version of themselves that doesn't square with what their potential employer had seen in the application. When what they should want is to be seen as the same, if not better. The only way to portray yourself better in a job interview is to portray yourself as more genuine. As old and cliche as it sounds, you have to be yourself.

That's where body language matters most. No one wants to hire someone that seems to have something to hide - and that is exactly how insecure people come off. No truth is worse than imagined lies. If you are down on yourself even while your potential employer is confident in your potential, they will begin to wonder if you know something about yourself that they do not.

Therefore, walk into the room with long, confident steps. Slow down, there is no rush - let them see that you know you belong in the room with them. This creates a level playing field. Some executives will try to see if they can ruffle your feathers, especially if the job you are applying for could involve a lot of stress. When or if they are doing that, let your body language show that you are not giving them the power to decide your future. If you walk into the room and give off an air of need, you are begging to be taken advantage of. They called you in because they see your potential - be like a football phenom deciding on a contract deal. You have the skill. You may have the need for money, but you can get money anywhere. They need your skills, and those are not always easy to come by.

When being evaluated, most people close themselves off. It isn't exactly fun to be under the microscope. But, it is a mistake to let them know it makes you uncomfortable. The more uncomfortable you seem, the more they will wonder if there is something you are hiding from them. Do not cross your arms or legs. Sit comfortably with your body open to them. Raise your head a little higher, to expose your neck. This shows immense confidence, as exposing the neck is - in essence - a show of comfort in vulnerability. You are giving them the chance to shoot right at you, and you are showing that you are not afraid.

Intimidation tactics are not unusual in job interviews. The most common tactic is strong eye contact. They will look straight at you and may even give you the illusion that only the two of you exist in that moment. This is a last resort of the interviewer to test your comfort in your own skin. If you look back at them with confidence or show no signs of being bothered by their stares, you are showing them that you are being transparent. You are the real deal, not a fake. This is exactly what every employer wants to believe about their employees. Show this strong body language and it significantly improves your chances of getting hired.

Date/Relationships

The reason there is more resistance in convincing someone to go on a date with you than getting an employer to hire you is because of what each group has to lose from a bad decision. Ultimately, how badly will it affect a company if they hire a poor worker? they will lose a bit of money, fire you, and then move on to better workers - right? If they hire you and you turn out not to be what you seemed to be at the start, the loss is almost entirely money-based - essentially, the bottom line decides whether you get to stay. Now compare that to the damage of bad love. Say that you date the person of interest and then, after they have formed feelings for you, everything goes south. What is lost then? Is it monetary? Not likely. It is emotional. And, how much emotional pain can someone afford to endure? No one truly knows, it depends on the person. The pain of a bad relationship can last years.

If you don't think that the person you plan to ask out is considering the ramifications of love gone sour, you are very naive. Almost everyone has had their heart broken and they don't, in any way, want to do it again.

Therefore, the most important thing to learn would have to be how to show your date that you won't hurt them the same, right? Actually, that's where things get interesting.

Fear of heartbreak is a very powerful thing. Like any phobia, it is not easily dissuaded. If someone is afraid of thunderstorms, you may try to assure them that the chances of getting struck by lightning are low - but so long as there is still a chance, this fact will not scare away the fear. Phobias are not tamed by words and assurances - they don't exist in the realm of plausibility; they lurk in the realm of possibility. You can use every logically valid argument you know to try to assure your date that you won't break their heart and they still won't believe you.

So, what then? Do you give up? Do you relent and just go shopping around for people who have never been let down or disappointed? No. That search won't yield too many results. You cannot assure a heart broken person that they will never be hurt again, just as you cannot assure someone playing out in the cold that they will never catch a cold doing so as they have in the past. So, what do you do?

You show them that you are worth the risk.

There is no success to be found in appealing to their fear, you must instead appeal to their curiosity. Potential pain or not, if you are able to intrigue your date, they will take the risk of being hurt again just to see what you are all about. Curiosity is the cure for fear, not comfort. Avoidance expands fear, curiosity ignores it.

So, then, what kind of body language can you show in order to create interest and intrigue when making the first impression on your date?

First, keep to the principles of what we covered in the job interview section. You must show them that you are confident in yourself and know you belong on the date with them. The more doubtful you are of yourself, the more doubtful she becomes about you too.

Next, you must use your skill with body language to speak to their subconscious more than their conscious. Why? Because it is the subconscious that is the worried one. It will repeat itself over and over, even after the date is over. On the conscious level, she might be excited and interested - but her subconscious, if it is not addressed, will negatively impact her view of you and your potential together. So, how do you speak with the subconscious? Indirectly, of course!

The subconscious plays upon the most vivid, strongest memories and experiences. Your conscious mind can only hold so much in mind at one time, but your subconscious can be aware of so much more. Everyday phrases and common experiences are easy to compute and ponder for the conscious mind, but it is the uncommon that sticks with the layer underneath. It is the same when it comes to body language.

There is a limit to how much we can touch others with our words. Many times, the best ways in which we can touch others is literally through touch. One of the best tactics for speaking straight to the subconscious rather than just to the conscious is to add touch. Lightly touch the arm as you are about to say something important and meaningful, for instance. This awakens the subconscious, forcing it to pay attention to your words with special focus and halt the conscious mind from its constant chatter.

Light, passing touches are a good way to create greater connection and make you more than just another person, but rather a part of the person you are speaking to. Dates go much smoother and are much more meaningful when you allow this connection to come to life. Be open, be interested, and be ready to connect - they will follow along.

Pickup/Negotiations

Next, we are going to discuss two different scenarios that essentially utilize the same body language skill set.

These scenarios being:

1) approaching a person of interest in order to ask them on a date
2) negotiating or haggling with a salesman or merchant.

Why are these two scenarios similar to each other? In both situations, you are approaching someone to convince them of giving you something they would not give away freely.

Unlike the job interview, you have not been contacted and offered an opportunity. Unlike behavior on a date, you have not been given passive permission to take charge and interact. In both the pickup and negotiations situation, you are approaching a person you do not know with the objective of gaining from them something they have not already offered. Body language in these situations is more vital than any of the words coming out of your mouth. Without proper body language, you might as well try to convince a resting boulder to budge out of your way.

In both situations, the biggest obstacle you have to overcome is forcing the stranger you are approaching to take you seriously. How do you do that? Start by having no hesitation. When approaching them, walk with longer, more self-assured steps. Don't rush toward them and don't hunch over. Stand up straight and lock your eyes on your target.

The most important tip for body language in this situation is to keep it all controlled and slow. Fast, jerky, or involuntary gestures or positioning signals to the person you are approaching that you are not prepared to do and say what is necessary to get what you want. If they don't believe that you believe you'll succeed, they will do everything in their power to make sure you don't.

With pickup, you want to know what you want and show it with your body language. The more self-assured and laid back you are, the more likely the person you are approaching will hear you out rather than immediately count you out. We teach people how to treat us, and we do this first and foremost throughout body language. Hold yourself with confidence and pride, and they will wonder exactly what it is about you that gives you so much gusto and cockiness. Go the other way by being insecure and intimidated and they will instead wonder about what you know about yourself that is making you act that way. Only bold confidence can get a stranger to give you a chance.

In negotiation, you have to be even more clever. You must equally position yourself as benign and friendly, while also showing that you won't be a pushover. Any salesman is going to want to get you to pay more than is necessary for what you want. It is your job, starting with your body language, to let them know that you are on to their game. Once again, confident body language is essential. However, you have to increase the volume, so to speak. Raise your head high and wear a knowing smile throughout negotiations and you will get a far better deal. The most reluctant con artist is the one that knows their victim is in on the game. Begin negotiations with open body language, then cross your arms when you have decided on the price you believe to be fair. This automatically signals to the merchant that you are not going to be easy to swindle.

Ultimately, body language is one of the most useful tools you have to show things that cannot be easily said. How do you say 'I am right for the job, stop fooling yourself and just hire me?' without setting off red alarms? You don't. You show it instead. How do you tell a date 'I'm not like everyone else, I'm worth the risk of heartbreak' - exactly, you don't! Those words mean nothing - but your body language, effectively showing instead of telling, means everything. Words have a distinct limitation to them that body language does not share.

Personality Types and Different Behavior Patterns

We have established the need for body language and what you stand to gain from putting to expert use the proper gestures in the proper situations. Now, in the next few chapters, we will delve further into the art of analyzing the body language of others. First, in this chapter, we will go over how to discover particular personality types from their body language habits. While this is not an exact science - because there are exceptions to every rule - the following information is useful as a means to make initial judgments and evaluations before getting to know the subject better.

Below, we have body language patterns for extroverts vs introverts, liars, and honest people, as well as those likely to be dangerous. The information given can be put to use both as a means to gain a grasp of others before approaching them, as well as a directory for warning signs that may keep you from approaching them at all. On its own, this chapter is only basic and is far from exact - but, coupled with the rest of the book, it is an irreplaceable, basic guide to analyzing the body language of strangers.

Extrovert vs. Introvert

Made more famous through the Meyers-Briggs personality evaluation than, perhaps, any other means, the terms 'extrovert' and 'introvert' describe the way individual interacts with the social world. One is not better than the other, they are just descriptors - similar to male and female. Both types have contributed greatly to the worlds of science, art, and politics. The importance of knowing an extrovert from an introvert is knowing how best to understand and interact with them, as the two types are quite different socially.

An extrovert is generally a more flamboyant, talkative, highly visible type - they thrive on being among people and interacting with them. In fact, at the end of a long work week, the one thing an extrovert wants to do most is get out of the house and do something. Interact with people, visit, party, that kind of thing.

An introvert is generally more reserved and more of an observer, and they are not as fond of the limelight as the extrovert is - they thrive on solitude and enjoying time doing the things they love. In other words, they are more likely to want to stay home and spend time with themselves or a smaller group of people than to attend parties. They need time away from the social world to recharge.

The biggest and most visible difference between the two groups is how much time they spend on their own. An introvert maintains their social life because they enjoy it as an activity and as a means for keeping friends and meeting people. An extrovert maintains their social life because they would go crazy without it. They are very social animals and hate spending too much time on their own.

So, how do we tell one from the other when we are just meeting them for the first time?

The difference in Personal Space: The first and most universal sign of introversion is that introverts have a bigger 'bubble' that they see as their personal space. They value their solitude so much that they take it with them, so to speak. You have to get a lot closer - proximity-wise - to an extrovert than an introvert in order to create a sense of intimacy.

Generally, given a room half-filled with people, the introvert will stand alone where there is space while an extrovert is attracted to where the people are.

Willingness to Touch: Extroverts are much more socially forward than introverts. This mostly being because being a socialite is almost inherent to being an extrovert, while it requires effort from an introvert. Extroverts tend to show their greater social aptitude by touching others more often. Touching your arm when speaking, patting you on the back, and even interacting with your hands. For most extroverts, they are just as social with their bodies as they are with their mouths.

This is a pretty steep contrast with the introvert, who is hesitant to touch. This is because, as we have established, the introvert has less desire to have people invading their space than the extrovert does. One thing to note when dealing with and understanding the body language of extroverts and introverts? They interact with others in the way that they want others to interact with them. When you understand the differences between the two, you can be an extrovert that makes good friends with introverts and vice versa. Without this knowledge, you will make the introvert feel invaded and you will convince the extrovert that you don't care for them.

Eye Contact: Contrary to popular thought, an extroverted person is not necessarily a confident person and an introverted person is not necessarily insecure. This is a common misconception mostly because of how each type sees the other. Introverts see extroverts running about making friends everywhere and they assume that they must be bold and confident - but that doesn't have to be the case at all. Vice versa, extroverts watch introverts keeping to themselves and assume they must be spending time alone because they don't have the confidence to play well with others. Both of these stereotypes are wrong, and actually very misleading.

For instance, which personality type would you imagine having stronger, more intense eye contact? A grand majority of people would think the extrovert would utilize better eye contact, but this is not the case. Introverts tend to, on average, show more connection through eye contact than their more social counterparts. Part of this is through necessity, as social interaction is a workout for introverts while it is more analogous to breathing when it comes to extroverts. How much do you have to focus in order to breathe? Not much, right?

Introverts tend to have stronger eye contact and sometimes are even more socially 'present' and are better listeners than their social butterfly opposites.

Idiosyncrasies: Where many - but not all - introverts reveal themselves. An idiosyncrasy, if you have never heard of it, is a particular bit of behavior which particularly stands out for being different and unique. Blinking, for instance, would not be an idiosyncrasy - but, blinking only one eye at a time is. Idiosyncrasies are loud because they are unusual. Not always weird or bizarre, but they stand out as uncorrected bits of human behavior or body language specific to a particular person. That person that believes he shouldn't wash his socks when he is on a streak of sports wins? he is got an idiosyncrasy. The one that is always mixing their metaphors? They have an idiosyncrasy. We all have idiosyncrasies, but guess which personality type shows it more?

That's right - introverts. And, it is obvious why. Extroverts, spending so much time getting to know new people and being social, are far more likely to have their idiosyncrasies noticed (and then corrected) than the more reserved introvert. There is even some evidence to show that introverts are less likely to correct idiosyncrasies when pointed out than extroverts are. This is likely because the introvert spends far more time by themselves and might value their opinion of themselves higher than extroverts. When you are a social animal, the social world has more power to influence you.

Liars vs. The Honest

If people can beat lie detectors, how can we hope to spot them lying with just our minds and our skills of observation? Well, let's begin by talking for a moment about lying. The reason why certain individuals are able to beat lie detectors is because, as you might well already know, a machine can't really detect if you are telling a lie. They can only detect specific bodily reactions that tend to happen when a person lies.

There are two types of people who regularly beat lie detectors - the confused and the amoral.

Will a lie detector be alerted if a man says he had pancakes on a morning he had waffles? Only if he knows he had waffles. If he truly believes he had pancakes, then he is technically being honest. Being honest and telling the truth are two different things. The truth is the objective, accurate version of what took place, while honesty is the subjective, possibly inaccurate version of what happened. In other words, a person cannot tell the truth and still not be lying.

Also, will the lie detector be alerted if a man tells a lie but has no moral aversion to doing so? Seeing as how many sociopaths have passed polygraphs, we would have to come to the conclusion that - no - the lie detector would remain silent.

Both situations tell us two important things that we have to consider when trying to spot a liar through body language.

- Honest does not mean true, it means not trying to deceive. You cannot know if another person is telling the truth, you can only know if they are trying to deceive you.
- A lie is most noticeable when the liar has an underlying knowledge that they are lying and that lying is wrong or risky.

This is why you will not see some of the more commonly taught 'tells' in this book. A tell is a body language cue that tips you off on the fact that the subject is lying. Some of the more commonly taught 'tells' are; touching of the nose, looking up and to the right before answering, and sweating. The reason this book is not putting an emphasis on these teachings is that they are very imperfect and are not proven.

Excessive itching of the nose can be far more a sign of allergies than lying. The looking up and to the right tell is only useful when the liar is unpracticed or has an awareness that they are telling a lie. And while excessive sweating can be a dependable 'tell', it can also indicate nervousness without guilt. Many people have been held in questioning for hours because the cops interrogating them figured their sweating was a sign of guilt, rather than fear of being mistakenly locked up. So, we have three more dependable 'tells' below, always to be put into context and not to be condemning evidence on their own.

Fidgeting: Not only nervous fidgeting, but all fidgeting should be scrutinized. Involuntary, automatic body and hand movements are often good signals about someone's inner state. The way in which they fidget can point to nervousness, deceitfulness, and excitement. The kind we are talking about here is the distracting, controlled kind. There are a lot of reasons for a stranger or someone you know to be nervous, there is no reason - without context - to assume their nervous fidgeting is a sign of being a liar. However, when the person you are speaking with picks something up and begins fooling with it, or starts fooling with their hands or clothes as they spin out an unlikely story yarn, it is often a sign of deceitful intent. People tend to habitually fidget more when they are listening. If they do a lot of fidgeting while talking, especially slow fidgeting that catches your attention, it is likely that they - like a magician - are using a distraction as a means to make you magically believe them.

As we will go over a few more times in this book, practiced liars tend to be identifiable through their over-eagerness or excessive acting. They are aware they are telling a lie, want to deceive you, and have practiced their story a few times, so to speak. Instead of the accidental tells shown by inexperienced liars, they are more detectable for excessively covering their tracks. In this case, the slow, attention-grabbing fidgeting is meant to make you believe they are at ease and relaxed, thus suggests their narrative is the truth. When called out for lying, it is normal for even an honest person to express irritation and anger - a totally cool and indifferent reaction is highly suspect.

Abnormal Blinking: Most practiced liars have heard that liars tend to blink more. Once again, this is a case of mistaking nervousness for lying. It certainly can be the case that a liar will blink more than your average person, but it is just as likely that the person you are speaking to is nervous for another reason, or simply blinks more than normal - maybe dry eye? The real 'tell' is when you noticed abnormal blinking. Most notably? Not blinking.

Like we mentioned already, practiced liars tend to overcorrect. They don't want you thinking they are telling a lie by blinking too much, so they try not to blink at all. Or, they go long periods without blinking, followed by excessive blinking. This suggests that they are aware of their blinking habits way more than any innocent person should be. An innocent person doesn't spend much time trying to avoid body language that could suggest they are lying. Attempting to seem honest is something only a liar has to dedicate time to. Without blinking, their eyes will become dry. To correct, they will have to blink more for a period. It is neither non-blinking or excessive blinking that is the tell, but abnormal blinking that suggests suspiciously excessive time spent thinking about how often to blink.

Exaggerated Gestures: Overcorrection is a big problem for even the most practiced liar. Often times, people are drawn in by exaggerated gestures because of the speaker's high level of charisma. Yet, if those same people spent even just a few minutes with a habitually honest person, they would notice something very different. Honest people use gestures and facial expressions big enough for one person to observe. Liars tend to gesticulate wildly as if speaking to a crowd. They try way too hard and that's why they get caught.

'Look into my eyes and tell me I am lying to you', and then they make their eyes bigger and stare into your soul. Sorry buddy, but you probably are lying. Honest people don't make a big show, they don't have to. They know they are not lying, they don't have much to prove. A liar has everything to prove. Overly precise, loud, calculated body language is always a significant sign that the user is trying to spin a tale. Just watch any practiced politician.

The Dangerous Ones

In most cases, you will know a dangerous person if you see one. They will have a weapon or be wearing a hateful face. But, what about when the dangerous ones are hidden among the rest of the population? How can we see them for what they are, or could become?

It is important, before describing the following body language patterns, that we establish that a 'dangerous one' is a wolf in sheep's clothing. We are not only talking about people who may become physically violent but people who - in general - are likely to give you trouble and reveal themselves to be different from the innocent, average person they portray in society.

Contradictory Body Language: Contradictory body language describes two different phenomena, both being suspicious and important to notice. The first is when the words spoken by someone reflect a different idea than that of their body language. For example, gritting the teeth while telling you they are happy you got the promotion. As a rule, body language always supersedes spoken language - one is calculated, one often isn't. The second is when the person is displaying body language that contradicts itself. For example, a warm smile while they squeeze their fists, white-knuckled, at their sides.

Noticing contradictory body language could be the difference between knowing people for who they are and being surprised with a dagger in your back.

Invasive/Forward-Learning Body Language: In the Western part of the world, especially, be wary of body language that reminds you of a snake getting ready to strike, or a cat getting ready to pounce. When people get into your space without warning, it is a potential threat. When you are seated opposite and they sit forward suddenly while arguing with you, it is time to cool things down. Aggression starts with the ready pose - and getting into your space is exactly how dangerous people prepare to attack.

Context always matters, but when it comes to contradictory body language and invasive body language, it is better to be wary and suspicious than to be gullible and assaulted.

General Body Language Examples

No body language guide is complete without providing a directory of different body languages cues and what truths they are likely to tell about the people using them. Always remember that no gesture tells the whole story without context, but any gesture can help you get started. Below, we have a humble listing of popular cues you can see every day. This is by no means a complete list, but it is an essential list. Becoming a master of body language, start by observing the cues listed here:

Feet and Legs

Toes pointed away - We all want to feel like our words are being listened to and that what we have to say is being listened to by the person we are speaking with. However, the worst time to want to be listened to is at a time where the listener has something else they want to do or somewhere else they want to be. How can you tell? Their toes will be pointed away from you, often toward their destination or toward the exit. Never start a serious conversation unless their toes are pointed straight at you.

Legs squeezed together - There are a few regions on the human body considered to be vulnerable zones. One of these areas is the neck, and another of these areas is the groin area. When a man or woman spends an excessive amount of time covering these areas, especially by squeezing their legs together, it can be a sign of nervousness and insecurity.

Crossed ankles behind them - It is a common gesture for men and women to cross their ankles to display comfort and relaxation. However, the opposite may actually be true if those crossed ankles and feet are hidden. E.g. under a chair or crossed beneath their rear. This is more a sign of attempted comfort in a situation the person considers to be stressful.

Jittery Legs - It won't surprise you too much to know that jittery legs - ones that have a tendency to bounce and wiggle a lot, tend to belong to people that are nervous or full of energy. This, however, could be an important tell when applied to a person who does not normally display this kind of body language.

Soles exposed - Exposure of the soles of the feet is a sign of confidence and ease. A person who has no problem putting their feet up, with their soles out toward you, is not a person who considers you a threat. The meaning of this gesture is made more obvious if the person is barefooted at the time, as the soles of the feet are another weak and vulnerable spot. Exposing your soles to a person is a sign that you are comfortable and do not fear them.

Chest and Shoulders

Crossed arms - we have mentioned it several times, but it is worth mentioning again because of its prevalence. When someone crosses their arms over their chest, they are either feeling attacked, are upset or resentful, or are cold. it is worth noting that some people consider this to be a comfortable pose and may use it for comfort - this is why it is important to apply context to every body language cue.

Hunched shoulders - Barring medical problems or natural hunching, shoulder hunches are more likely to have lower self-esteem and a lower sense of pride. This does not always show immediately - as a person with hunched shoulders may portray themselves as a confident person that just doesn't care. The fact remains, people with pride and self-esteem tend to stand upright, not hunched.

Puffed Chest - A puffed out chest is your best and most reliable sign of someone's confidence. Not just humans, but most primates puff their chests for the same reason a cat puffs up its hair - to appear strong and virile, and like a beast you would not want to mess with. Some people have naturally pronounced chests, but notice those who stand tall and upright, with chests puffed and rugged. These are the people with the highest amounts of pride. Confident or not, these people will act the part well.

Diagonal Alignment - When someone is standing or seated across from you and their torso is in a diagonal alignment rather than squared in your direction, it is a similar cue to that of the person whose toes point elsewhere. They are not totally invested in conversing with you. Different with this cue, however, is that it may imply they are not interested in conversing with you because they have something to hide. A good way to remember this is crooked shoulders equals crooked intentions.

Consistent Shoulder Adjustment - Ever been talking with someone who keeps adjusting their shoulders? Don't worry. This is a nervous gesture that is most common in people with anxiety disorders, as it relates to an overactive awareness of their body and its uncomfortable positioning.

Hands and Fingers

White Knuckled Fist - White knuckling is a sign of powerful aggression. A benign, relaxed fist will not display whitened knuckles, but a fist expressing anger, frustration, or aggression will be obvious from its whitened knuckles. People displaying this gesture are to be watched carefully. It may be that they are in pain or uncomfortable, but it may also signify hostility and possibility of aggression.

Open palms - When gesturing, people reveal a lot about their nature. For instance, a person that is open and guilt free will often gesticulate with open palms. That is, palms so that you can see them. The palms, like the soles of the feet, the neck, and the groin region, are a soft, vulnerable spot on the human body. When a person exposes them regularly, it is a sign that they are not afraid to be open and honest, and have little to hide.

Wringing - Fidgeting is something to always have your eye on because it displays involuntary, subconscious behavior. Wringing, however, displays something quite different from the more erratic, nervous fidgeting that you will be exposed to. Wringing is a self-soothing bit of body language. It arises when someone is worried or highly upset and their subconscious tries to comfort them and keep them calm.

Knuckle Cracking - Many people crack their knuckles out of habit because of discomfort in their knuckles. A person who does not naturally do this and cracks their knuckles, however, may be attempting to intimidate.

Eye Contact

Consistent Downward Looks - Eye contact isn't something that you have to maintain without breaking - that's just staring. However, a person that consistently breaks eye contact by looking down and away is likely to have something hide. Most often it is that they are bashful and may be attracted to you, but it can also be a sign of guilt.

Avoidance of Eye Contact - It will sound completely unscientific, but it is a fact that some people are just really weird. If you ever meet someone who doesn't use much eye contact, they might just be a little different, so to speak... but it might also mean they are afraid of what you will see in them if they look into your eyes.

Strained Eye Contact - When someone is forcing themselves to maintain eye contact, it is highly suspect. Why are they trying so hard to look normal? What is it that they could be hiding, beyond their bloodshot, tear-filled eyes?

Abnormal Blinking - This relates to strained eye contact, as we discussed earlier. Blinking excessively and not blinking a lot are not, on their own, signs of anything in particular. However, intermittently going from not blinking at all, to blinking a lot? That's something to watch. As is forced blinking. Some people are all-too-aware of the effects that eye contact and blinking can have when making an impression on someone. They try to correct this by blinking in a perfect rhythm. These people, funny enough, tend to be outed because they spend so much time trying to blink properly that the rest of their body language is blank.

Posture/Positioning

Curved Spine - Barring medical causes, a person that spends too much time bent over - especially while standing - is very likely to suffer from depression and low self-esteem. Much like the hunched shoulders, a curved spine can be a signifier that the person has a low view of themselves and is without much pride.

Rigid Spine - On the opposite end you have those that stand ridiculously straight, almost to the point where it seems to be paining them. Would you be surprised to know that people with exaggerated uprightness tend to suffer from the same things as those with curved spines? Just like the liar trying to seem like the beacon of truth, people with low self-esteem sometimes try to fake confidence. However, like the liar, they overcorrect and end up looking pretty conspicuous - which is the opposite of their intent.

Personal Space - Introverts and extroverts need different amounts of personal space. While the extrovert is often comfortable with touch and casual spacial intimacy, the introvert is just the opposite. It is easy to detect one from the other by seeing how they react to you. Stand right next to them when there is room for you to have more space - an extrovert will barely notice and may even chat you up. An introvert will make space for themselves.

Spreading - Confident people take up space. You will not see a proud, high self-esteem person being crushed into a corner while everyone else can spread out. Confident people may even take up 'too much space' at times. They will sit down at a table - sit down in one chair and use the other two to rest their arms. Meanwhile, the insecure person shies away from this, preferring to take up very little space as to avoid inconveniencing others.

Facial Expressions

Eye-Involved Smiling - How do you tell a genuine smile from a fake smile? Genuine smiles make better use of the eyes. A person smiling to be friendly will look mostly the same from the nose up, even while their mouth is curled into a grin.

Impossible to be Disgusted with a Smile - If you approach someone and you are talking with them, and they act like something you said or did disgusted them, look at their whole face. The facial expression for disgust is very exaggerated. You cannot react in disgust and smile at the same time. If they say you are disgusting but smile, they are very likely to be teasing you rather than mean it literally.

True Fear - People often look to the eyes in order to discover whether or not someone is genuinely afraid. This is a bad move. The eyes are limited in what they can express. Much more reliable is the neck. When someone is genuinely startled or afraid, their neck will take on exaggerated shapes. The cords of the neck may become pronounced and rigid, and the area just below Adam's apple stands out as well.

Gestures

Wild arm movement - Wild/Rapid arm and hand movement signify two things. One is anger and frustration, maybe even fear. The other is low confidence. Calm, confident people use slower, controlled gestures. Heated, fearful, insecure people tend to use fast, wild gestures.

Backhanded - The opposite of the open palm is the back of the hand, and it is the part of the hand that is shown by those that have something to hide or are afraid to be challenged. They will gesture at you with the back of their hand, not exposing their palm. This symbolizes a very real unwillingness to expose their true selves and true intentions.

Talking with Hands - Ever wanted to know if someone was likely to be a creative type? Chat with them for a few minutes. In general, but especially when passionate, creative types tend to talk as much with their hands as they do with their mouths. This is because they are creator types. Their desire to express and help you understand their expressions leads to them utilizing much more body language and gesturing than their less creative counterparts.

Methods and Techniques to Analyze People

If you are like most researchers delving into the world of body language, this is the chapter you bought the book for. You want to know how to read people, using the knowledge of body language to become a human lie detector and Holmesian deductive sleuth. No worries! That's an excellent goal to have, and it is an achievable one at that - with the knowledge we have gained throughout these chapters, plus the knowledge you are about to receive, there will be few people able to hide their intentions and true feelings from you. Lies will be transparent, personalities will be loud and visible, and you will have everything you need in order to make body language ensure your success in business, in relationships, and in life.

But, before you go off to conquer the world, we have a few final and very vital aspects to learn about the art of reading body language. Without these tools, your learning is incomplete - so, please, if you only take a few concepts to heart once you have finished this book, let them be the concepts below.

Establishing the Norms Through Observation

Context: it is a word we have used several times in this book, and for good reason. Just as good words can be made to sound careless out of context, body language loses the bulk of its meaning when removed from the situations in which it arises.

Take for instance the simple crossing of the arms. Now, as we have learned, crossing your arms is a significant act which can show others that you are closed off to communicating or connecting. Most often, it is a sign of insecurity, resentment, or underlying aggression. However, what happens when we take our cross-armed person and place them in a winter wonderland with no coat? We now have another valid reason for them to have their arms crossed - they are cold!

Another example: We have, to this point, associated good posture and a raised chin with confidence and self-esteem. Therefore, if we see someone that is significantly slouched with their chin tucked into their chest, we have good reason to suspect that they are not the confident type but are rather quite insecure, or even depressed. This isn't always the case, but it is certainly a valid deduction given the lack of pride showing from their body language. However, what happens when we find out that this person has not slept in thirty-six hours and is completely exhausted? Once again, we have another valid reason for them to be displaying this particular form of body language. They could be the most confident person in the land, but everyone is bound to slouch when they are tired!

We might suspect the nose itcher of lying when they have just got a case of the sniffles. We might think the rapid blinker is nervous, but perhaps they have a bad case of dry eye? And, as we discussed in the first chapter, we might suspect that a man standing before us, nose-to-nose, is a threat when in fact it might just be their cultural custom.

All of this amounts to the number one rule of body language. You cannot deduce with certainty until you have established what is 'normal'. You can't expose a liar for itching their nose too much if they are a constant nose itcher. To be absolutely certain of whether someone is lying, you must first know the body language displayed when they are honest.

Through your ability to detect honesty, you will be freed to see through their deception. This leads us to the first step you must take to broaden your ability to deduce through body language - observing others, making note of their body language, and applying it to different situations. Only once you have established the 'tells' for a particular person can you be certain that they are lying about something vital.

Discover the Individual Body Language of Those You Know, Associated with Situations

To get started, begin with just one person. It could be a family member, a coworker, or a friend. This person is going to become your test subject. Through them you will gain greater deductive power, and you will understand the powerful truths you can learn by observing body language. Let's work with a few examples:

First, let's say that you have chosen a coworker and you would like to gain greater understanding of when they are being genuinely friendly vs. when they are faking it. Your first step has to be to observe them. Establish in your mind the people that he or she likes and who he or she does not. Watch the interactions play out between these two groups. Now, it could be simple. Your coworker might be obviously friendly with those he or she likes and obviously hostile with those he or she does not. A friendly smile and open body language vs crossed arms and a disgusted scowl.

However, if you work in a public job that requires constant interaction with customers, it is unlikely that your coworkers will feel free to express their hostility in such a free, uninhibited manner. Instead, they will become passive-aggressive - showing a friendly front whilst having hidden hostile emotions. This is the more tricky person to uncover, but, with the skills you have gained from this book, you will undoubtedly discover their hidden nature.

You might notice how they react when a person they like asks them to do something they resent. This will create a mismatching of emotions and interesting body language will arise out of that. Once you have seen how their body expresses this contradiction of feelings, you will have an idea of what they look like when they are putting on a friendly front but are not feeling so friendly underneath.

Another example: Let's say you are flirting with someone and you'd really like to know if they are attracted to you or not. A mistake made by many, both men and women, is to assume that certain gestures and certain body language automatically signals interest. While there are some promising signs that can be observed through body language, you cannot know for sure if these signs are part of their natural body language or are being shown special for you. That is, unless you observe and establish the norms first.

Some people are very naturally flirtatious, and their body language will show it. They have open postures, expose their neck, smirk a little, and seem to undress you with their eyes. Sadly, if they are using this form of body language with everyone, you cannot assume that they are attracted if they begin using this body language while talking to you.

Instead, you have to pay special attention to the flirtatious body language they don't use on everyone. Maybe they reserve the old lip bite or fluttering eyes for special cases - you have not seen them being used on everyone else. So, when she starts using them on you, the chance that she is attracted to you is much higher than if she used only her normal flirting gestures.

One more example: You have high suspicions that someone in your life has been lying to you. It could be your boss or your employee, it could be a member of your family, a friend, or a lover. Whoever it is, you know that it is in your best interest to know for sure if they are lying to you. From there, you can decide what to do next - whether to forgive and forget or not. But, first, you have to ascertain if your suspicions are accurate.

So, you observe them. You take note of their natural body language. Maybe you even get sneaky by asking them a question you know they will fib about, and then seeing the body language they use when they are lying to you. All priming yourself for the opportunity to question them. When you have an individual accounting for the body language someone uses when they are lying about one thing, it proves helpful in revealing to you when they are lying about anything.

Pay Special Attention to Non-Necessary, Compulsory Body Language e.g. fidgeting

Not all body language can be faked

To this point, we have had to recognize two different causes for body language analysis inaccuracy.

 Those two being

- Body language can be learned and practiced, and
- Idiosyncrasies and context.

However, as there always is, there is an exception to the rule. The exception? Fidgeting.

It is a part of body language that is incredibly difficult to fake genuinely, and which has few uses other than to express what is going on inside someone subconsciously.

Fidgeting is subconscious

Most always, we fidget subconsciously. We don't even realize we are doing it until someone points it out, or something wakes us from our internal banter. However, it may interest you to know that actors - who will fidget on purpose - often end up with the mental state and feelings related to fidgeting. In other words, if they are playing a character that fidgets because they are nervous, the actor finds themselves becoming nervous the more they act it out. Thus, it is fairly irrelevant whether the intention or the feeling comes first. If a person is fidgeting, it is a significant sign of what is going on beyond their conscious mind.

Take for example, in an interrogation: When the officers come into the room to interrogate the suspect, they don't have to think as hard about the context of the suspect's body language when he begins to fidget nervously. It just tells them that he is nervous. A suspect that fidgets in a particular way for a decent amount of time is likely to just be nervous, regardless of their guilt or innocence. But when the fidgeting starts and stops and changes and interrupts another fidgeting, it is a cue showing the cops that the suspect is unsure of himself. And, to their minds, why would an innocent man be unsure of himself?

Your Free Gift

I wanted to express my appreciation that you support my work so I've put together a free gift for you

31 Healthy Smoothie recipes for month

Just visit the link above to download it now.

I'm sure you will love this gift.

Thanks!

*Link to download book

http://publish4you.wixsite.com/ebook-gift

www.ingramcontent.com/pod-product-compliance
Lightning Source LLC
Chambersburg PA
CBHW070235290526
45789CB00004B/1635